ORIENTAL

1998 Published by Rebo Productions Ltd., London.
Designed and created by Consortium, England

Typeset by MATS, Southend-on-Sea, Essex
Edited by Anne Sheasby
Ceres Verlag recipes compiled and translated
by Stephen Challacombe
Illustrations by Camilla Sopwith

J0247UK
Cover design: Minkowsky, The Netherlands

Printed in Slovenia

ISBN 1 84053 135 5

ORIENTAL

EXOTIC YET QUICK AND EASY DISHES FOR EVERY OCASION

Contents

Introduction

Oriental cooking is not a single cuisine but rather a culinary style which draws on the wide range of cooking traditions from China, Japan, Thailand, Indonesia, Malaysia, Indonesia, the Philippines and India, to produce exciting and exotic dishes with imaginative combinations of ingredients and flavourings.

There are many elements common to the individual indigenous cuisines of the Orient. There is a strong emphasis on using fresh produce, and vegetables play a central role in most savoury dishes, as do fresh fruits in desserts. A whole variety of flavours are finely balanced between sweet and sour, fragrant and hot through the subtle combining of fresh herbs, sauces, spices and other seasonings. The staples of rice and noodles are also key ingredients, providing the basis of main courses and side dishes or supplementing other dishes, such as soups.

Many of the specialist ingredients used in Oriental cooking are now readily available from major supermarkets, but Oriental food stores will generally stock all that you require.

Stir-frying is a prominent cooking method in the preparation of Oriental dishes. Both ultra-quick and easy, stir-frying is also a healthy way to cook, in that a minimum of oil is used in the process and nutrients are sealed into the food in its few minutes of cooking. Invest in a good-quality wok or use a large frying pan.

The recipes specially selected for this book reflect all the richness and variety of their Eastern origins and influences. Many of the featured dishes offer inspired, easy and speedy choices for everyday meals, including satisfying vegetarian options. In addition, there are more involved, sumptuous creations for entertaining and celebrations – some made extra-easy by adaptation to microwave cooking. Whatever the occasion, the dishes you choose are sure to stimulate and delight the eye as well as the tastebuds.

Philippine Pancakes

These light Oriental-style pancakes are filled with a delicious vegetable and lean beef mixture.

Preparation time: 20 minutes • Cooking time: 20 minutes • Serves: 4 (2 pancakes per serving)

Ingredients

For the pancakes

100 g (3½ oz) plain flour
15 ml (1 tbsp) cornflour
A pinch of salt
3 eggs
125 ml (4 fl oz) milk
30 ml (2 tbsp) melted butter

For the filling

30 ml (2 tbsp) vegetable oil
200 g (7 oz) fillet of beef, cut into thin strips
200 g (7 oz) French beans, trimmed and halved
1 carrot, thinly sliced
1 small leek, thinly sliced
200 g (7 oz) bamboo shoots, thinly sliced
8 Iceberg lettuce leaves

For the sauce

125 ml (4 fl oz) meat stock
15 ml (1 tbsp) sugar
15 ml (1 tbsp) soy sauce
15 ml (1 tbsp) wine vinegar
1.25 ml (¼ tsp) salt
5 ml (1 tsp) cornflour

Method

1
For the pancakes, mix together the flour, cornflour and salt in a bowl, then gradually beat in the eggs and milk, until a smooth batter is formed.

2
Heat the butter in an 18-cm (7-in) frying pan and pour in enough batter to thinly coat the base. Cook until golden brown, turn and cook the second side until golden. Place on a plate and keep hot. Repeat with the remaining batter to make 8 pancakes. Keep hot.

3
For the filling, heat the oil in a wok. Add the beef and stir-fry until brown all over. Add the beans, carrot, leek and bamboo shoots and stir-fry for about 3 minutes, until just softened. Remove from the heat and keep hot.

4
Wash the lettuce leaves and lay them on the pancakes, spread the beef and vegetable mixture over the top and roll the pancakes up. Keep hot.

5
For the sauce, place the stock in a pan with the sugar, soy sauce, wine vinegar and salt and bring to the boil. Blend the cornflour with 15 ml (1 tbsp) cold water and stir into the sauce. Cook until thickened, stirring. Simmer for 2 minutes. Pour the hot sauce over the pancakes to serve.

Serving suggestion

Serve with a mixed watercress and sliced tomato garnish.

Variations

Use 1 small onion in place of the leek. Use half white and half buckwheat or wholemeal flour for the pancakes.

Cook's tip

To keep pancakes separate and hot, pile cooked pancakes on top of each other with greaseproof paper in between. Keep hot in a low-medium oven.

Son-in-Law Eggs

This popular and well-known Thai dish is traditionally made with duck eggs, but hen eggs can be used instead.

Preparation time: 20 minutes • Cooking time: 20 minutes • Serves: 4

Ingredients

For the sauce

150 ml (¼ pint) tamarind juice *(see 'Cook's tip', page 32)*

70 g (2½ oz) dark muscovado sugar

90 ml (6 tbsp) fish sauce

Vegetable oil, for deep-frying

4 shallots, thinly sliced

4 cloves garlic, thinly sliced

4 hard-boiled eggs, peeled

Chilli flowers and spring onion brushes *(see 'Cook's tip')*, *to garnish*

Method

1
Combine the sauce ingredients in a small saucepan and heat gently, stirring, until the sugar dissolves. Bring to the boil, then reduce the heat and simmer gently for 5-10 minutes.

2
Meanwhile, heat the oil in a wok to 180°C/350°F. Add the shallots and fry for 1-2 minutes, until golden brown and crisp. Remove with a slotted spoon and drain on absorbent kitchen paper.

3
Add the garlic and fry for 1 minute, until pale golden, taking care not to allow it to burn. Remove with a slotted spoon and drain on absorbent kitchen paper.

4
Add the eggs to the wok and deep-fry for 5-10 minutes, until golden and bubbly all over. Keep turning the eggs so that they do not burn on the bottom. When golden, remove from the oil using a slotted spoon and drain the eggs on absorbent kitchen paper.

5
Cut the eggs in half lengthways and arrange on a serving plate. Sprinkle the fried shallots and garlic over the eggs. Serve the sauce in a separate bowl, or poured over the eggs. Garnish with chilli flowers and spring onion brushes and serve.

Serving suggestion

Serve with thick slices of fresh crusty bread.

Variations

Use quail's eggs in place of hen's eggs. Allow 2-3 per serving. Use 1 small onion in place of the shallots.

Cook's tip

To make chilli flowers, holding a chilli at its stem, slice open lengthways and remove the seeds. Cut through the chilli a few times just below the stem to the tip. Place in a bowl of iced water for about 1 hour. The ends of the chilli will curl outwards. Spring onion brushes are made in the same way. Trim away the root and the top of the green part, to leave a length about 5-7 cm (2-3 in). Make cuts from just below the root end to the green end, and place in iced water to make the green ends curl.

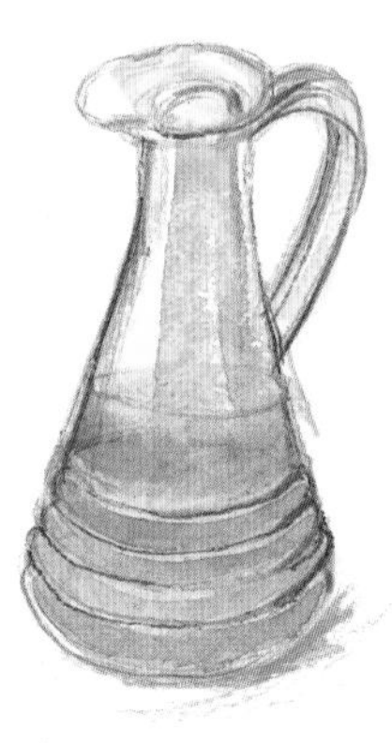

Thai Pork-Stuffed Omelettes

Plain omelettes filled with a spicy pork mixture make a delicious snack or starter.

Preparation time: 15 minutes • Cooking time: 20 minutes • Serves: 2

Ingredients

For the filling

30 ml (2 tbsp) vegetable oil
1 small green chilli, sliced
1 clove garlic, crushed
2 shallots, chopped
115 g (4 oz) minced pork
25 g (1 oz) shelled prawns, chopped
30 ml (2 tbsp) fish sauce
1 large plum tomato, chopped
10 ml (2 tsp) sugar
A pinch of white pepper
30 ml (2 tbsp) chopped fresh coriander

For the omelettes

4 eggs
15 ml (1 tbsp) fish sauce
30 ml (2 tbsp) vegetable oil
Chilli flowers (see 'Cook's tip', page 10), *to garnish*

Method

1
To make the filling, heat the oil in a frying pan or wok and fry the chilli, garlic and shallots for 3 minutes, or until softened.

2
Add the minced pork and cook until it has changed colour, breaking it up as it cooks.

3
Add the remaining filling ingredients and stir-fry for 3-4 minutes. Remove from the heat and keep warm while cooking the omelettes.

4
To make the omelettes, place the eggs in a mixing bowl with the fish sauce and 5 ml (1 tsp) water and whisk until well combined and slightly frothy.

5
Heat half the oil in a small heavy-based frying pan and when just hazing, pour in half the egg mixture. Reduce the heat and cook the egg mixture, pulling the egg from the side of the pan as it sets, and letting the uncooked mixture run to the edges of the pan.

6
When the egg mixture is almost set, gently flip over to cook the top, or place under a preheated grill to brown.

7
Spoon half the pork mixture onto the centre of the omelette and fold up to completely enclose. Transfer to a serving dish and keep warm.

8
Make and fill a second omelette with the remaining egg and pork mixture. Serve garnished with chilli flowers.

Serving suggestion
Serve with a hot and spicy dipping sauce.

Variations
Use minced beef or chicken in place of pork.

Cook's tip
If you have 2 small frying pans, cook both omelettes at once.

Ham and Egg Soup

A tasty yet quick and easy-to-prepare soup – ideal for a starter to an Oriental meal.

Preparation time: 10 minutes • Cooking time: 8-10 minutes • Serves: 4

Ingredients

55 g (2 oz) boiled lean ham
2 spring onions
1 litre (1¾ pints) chicken stock
3 eggs
15 ml (1 tbsp) soy sauce
5 ml (1 tsp) sesame oil
Freshly ground black pepper
Fresh herb sprigs, to garnish

Method

1

Slice the ham into thin strips, then clean and trim the spring onions and slice them into very fine rings. Set aside.

2

Place the stock in a saucepan and bring to the boil.

3

Lightly beat the eggs, soy sauce, sesame oil and pepper together and pour through a sieve into the boiling stock.

4

Remove from the heat and add the ham and spring onions. Leave to heat briefly in the hot stock, then ladle into warmed soup bowls to serve. Garnish with fresh herb sprigs.

Serving suggestion

Serve with crusty bread rolls or a French baguette.

Variations

Use smoked ham in place of unsmoked ham. Use vegetable stock in place of chicken stock.

Won-Ton Soup

A classic, substantial Chinese soup.

Preparation time: 30 minutes, plus 1 hour standing time • Cooking time: 40 minutes • Serves: 6

Ingredients

250 g (9 oz) plain wholemeal flour
2 eggs
A pinch of salt
A pinch of saffron
15 ml (1 tbsp) butter
300 g (10½ oz) skinless, boneless turkey, cut into thin strips
1 onion, finely chopped
200 g (7 oz) Chinese cabbage, shredded
1 small red pepper, seeded and sliced
1 clove garlic, thinly sliced
½ pear seasoned with mustard seeds, chopped
115 g (4 oz) bean sprouts
30 ml (2 tbsp) chives
Sambal oelek
Soy sauce
1.5 litres (2¾ pints) hot vegetable stock

Method

1
In a bowl, mix the flour, eggs, 75 ml (5 tbsp) water, salt and saffron together to form a stiff but kneadable dough and cover with cling film. Leave to rest for 1 hour at room temperature.

2
To make the filling, heat the butter in a pan and brown the turkey all over. Add the onion, cabbage and red pepper and cook for about 10 minutes, stirring continuously until all the juices have evaporated.

3
Add the garlic, pear, bean sprouts, chives and sambal oelek and soy sauce to taste, and stir to mix. Remove the pan from the heat and set aside.

4
Sprinkle flour on a clean tea-towel and roll out the won-ton dough until very thin. Cut into 10-cm (4-in) squares and place about 15 ml (1 tbsp) filling on each square of dough. Pull the sides of the dough together and press to close. Steam over a pan of boiling water for 20-25 minutes, until cooked.

5
Stir the cooked hot won-tons into the hot vegetable stock and ladle into warmed soup bowls to serve.

Serving suggestion
Serve with thin slices of toast.

Variations
Use plain white flour in place of wholemeal flour. Use chicken or pork in place of turkey.

Cook's tip
Sambal oelek is an Oriental chilli sauce. It is available from Oriental food stores.

Rice Soup with Pork

This unusual soup is of Thai origins. Traditionally, an egg is lightly poached in the soup just before serving.

Preparation time: 10 minutes • Cooking time: 20 minutes • Serves: 4

Ingredients

30 ml (2 tbsp) vegetable oil
2 cloves garlic, chopped
850 ml (1½ pints) pork or chicken stock
225 g (8 oz) minced pork
350 g (12 oz) cooked rice
2 sticks celery, sliced
2 spring onions, sliced
15 ml (1 tbsp) chopped fresh coriander
15 ml (1 tbsp) fish sauce
A pinch of white pepper

Method

1
Heat the oil in a small frying pan or wok and fry the garlic until pale golden. Remove with a slotted spoon and drain on absorbent kitchen paper.

2
Place the stock in a large saucepan and bring to the boil. Add the pork, rice, celery and spring onions and simmer gently for 15 minutes, stirring occasionally.

3
Stir in the coriander, fish sauce and pepper. Serve sprinkled with the fried garlic.

Serving suggestion

Serve with rice crackers.

Variation

Use chicken in place of pork and chop finely by hand or in a food processor.

Cook's tip

Fish sauce is widely used in Oriental cooking and eliminates the need for salt. It is available from Oriental food stores and many supermarkets. However, if unavailable, make your own substitute by pounding together canned anchovy fillets with a little sugar. Add a few spoonfuls of soy sauce and allow to stand for at least 30 minutes. Strain before using.

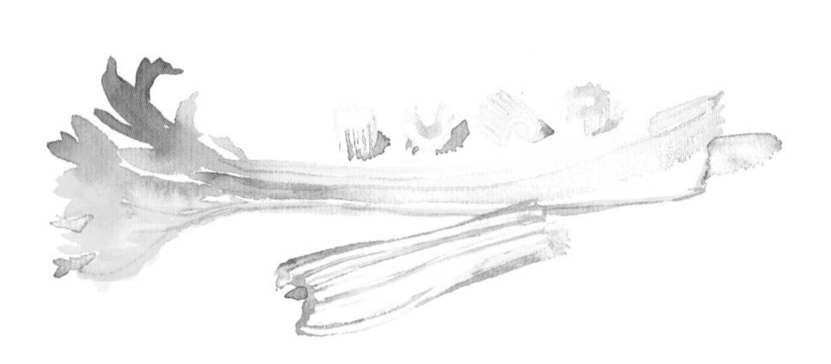

Chicken Coconut Soup

This is a wonderfully rich aromatic soup of medium chilli-heat.

Preparation time: 15 minutes • Cooking time: 20 minutes • Serves: 4

Ingredients

1 chicken breast, skinned and boned

425 ml (¾ pint) thick coconut milk *(see 'Cook's tip', page 40)*

300 ml (½ pint) chicken stock

6 slices galangal

2 red chillies, seeded and cut into strips

6 black peppercorns, crushed

4 kaffir lime leaves, torn in half

1 stem lemon grass, bruised

60 ml (4 tbsp) fish sauce

60 ml (4 tbsp) lime juice

Method

1
Cut the chicken into thin strips across the grain using a sharp knife. Set aside.

2
Combine the coconut milk and chicken stock in a large saucepan and bring to the boil.

3
Reduce the heat to a simmer and add the chicken, galangal, chillies, peppercorns, lime leaves and lemon grass. Simmer gently for 15-20 minutes, or until the chicken is tender and cooked through, stirring occasionally.

4
Stir in the fish sauce and lime juice and ladle into warmed soup bowls to serve.

Serving suggestion

Serve with thick slices of fresh crusty bread.

Variations

Use turkey in place of chicken. Use lemon juice in place of lime juice.

Cook's tip

Galangal is closely related to ginger and is similar in appearance but has a milder, more perfumed flavour. It is available fresh or dried from Oriental food stores. If unavailable, substitute ginger.

Hot and Sour Seafood Soup

This interesting combination of flavours and ingredients makes a sophisticated beginning to an informal meal.

Preparation time: 20 minutes • Cooking time: 20 minutes • Serves: 4

Ingredients

3 dried Chinese mushrooms

15 ml (1 tbsp) vegetable oil

115 g (4 oz) prawns or shrimps, shelled and deveined

1 red chilli, seeded and finely sliced

1 green chilli, seeded and finely sliced

2.5 ml (1/2 tsp) lemon rind, cut into thin slivers

2 spring onions, sliced

600 ml (1 pint) fish stock

15 ml (1 tbsp) Worcestershire sauce

15 ml (1 tbsp) light soy sauce

Salt and freshly ground black pepper

55 g (2 oz) white fish fillets

225 g (8 oz) bean curd (tofu), diced

15 ml (1 tbsp) lemon juice

5 ml (1 tsp) sesame seeds

5 ml (1 tsp) finely chopped fresh coriander

Method

1
Soak the mushrooms in enough hot water to cover for 20 minutes, or until completely reconstituted.

2
Heat the oil in a large wok or frying pan and add the prawns, chillies, lemon rind and spring onions. Stir-fry quickly for 1 minute.

3
Add the stock, Worcestershire sauce and soy sauce. Bring to the boil, reduce the heat and simmer for 5 minutes. Season to taste.

4
Remove the hard stalks from the mushrooms and discard. Slice the caps very finely.

5
Cut the fish fillets into small dice and add to the soup together with the bean curd and Chinese mushrooms.
Simmer for a further 5 minutes.

6
Stir in the lemon juice and sesame seeds. Adjust the seasoning and serve sprinkled with chopped fresh coriander.

Serving suggestion

Serve with rice or prawn crackers or thin slices of toast.

Variations

Use salmon or tuna in place of white fish. Use poppy seeds in place of sesame seeds.

Cook's tip

Care must be taken when using fresh chillies not to get the juice into the eyes or the mouth.
If this should happen, rinse them with lots of cold water.

Miso Soup

This delicious, healthy soup is of Japanese origin.

Preparation time: 15 minutes • Cooking time: 20 minutes • Serves: 2

Ingredients

1 small onion, grated

2.5-cm (1-in) piece root ginger, peeled and finely chopped

1 clove garlic, crushed

15 ml (1 tbsp) sesame oil

1 carrot, peeled and thinly sliced

¼ cauliflower, broken into florets

20 ml (1 large tbsp) arame (Japanese seaweed)

25 g (1 oz) peas (fresh or frozen)

30 ml (2 tbsp) shoyu (Japanese soy sauce)

15 ml (1 tbsp) miso (red bean paste)

Freshly ground black pepper, to taste

2 spring onions, finely chopped

Method

1. In a saucepan, gently fry the onion, ginger, and garlic in the sesame oil for a few minutes.
2. Add the carrot and cauliflower and gently sweat the vegetables for 5 minutes, stirring occasionally.
3. Add 1.2 litres (2 pints) water, arame, peas and shoyu and stir to mix. Cook for 15-20 minutes, until the vegetables are soft, stirring occasionally.
4. Blend the miso to a paste with a little of the soup liquid and add to the soup, but do not allow to boil.
5. Season to taste with pepper.
6. Ladle into warmed soup bowls and serve garnished with chopped spring onions.

Serving suggestion

Serve with hot garlic bread.

Variations

Substitute other vegetables such as turnip, swede, mangetout or green beans but remember that this soup is mainly a broth with a few floating vegetables. Use vegetable or chicken stock in place of water.

Cook's tip

Arame, shoyu and miso are available from Oriental food stores.

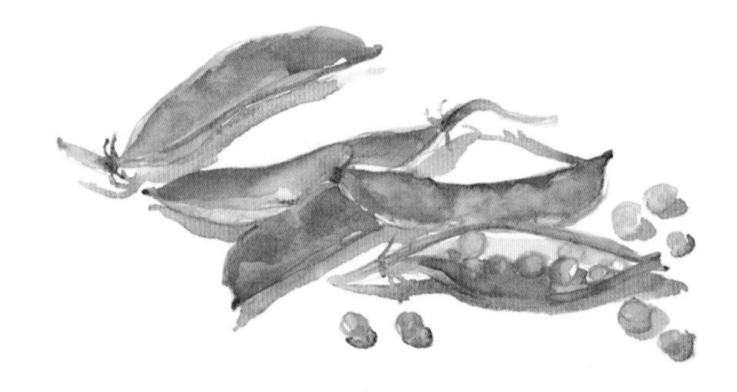

Coconut Fried Fish with Chillies

These pieces of crisp coconut-coated fish are served with a piquant, spicy sauce for dipping.

Preparation time: 30 minutes • Cooking time: 30 minutes • Serves: 4

Ingredients

Vegetable oil, for frying

450 g (1 lb) sole or plaice fillets, skinned, boned and cut into 2.5-cm (1-in) strips

Seasoned plain flour

1 egg, beaten

55 g (2 oz) desiccated coconut

15 ml (1 tbsp) sunflower oil

5 ml (1 tsp) grated root ginger

1 red chilli, seeded and finely chopped

1.25 ml (1/4 tsp) chilli powder

5 ml (1 tsp) ground coriander

2.5 ml (1/2 tsp) ground nutmeg

1 clove garlic, crushed

30 ml (2 tbsp) tomato purée

30 ml (2 tbsp) tomato chutney

30 ml (2 tbsp) dark soy sauce

30 ml (2 tbsp) lemon juice

30 ml (2 tbsp) water

5 ml (1 tsp) brown sugar

Salt and freshly ground black pepper

Method

1
In a frying pan, heat about 5 cm (2 in) of the vegetable oil to 190°C/375°F. Toss the fish strips in the seasoned flour, then dip into the beaten egg. Roll in the desiccated coconut and shake off the excess.

2
Fry the fish, a few pieces at a time, in the hot oil, then drain on absorbent kitchen paper. Set aside and keep warm.

3
Heat the sunflower oil in a wok or frying pan and fry the ginger, chilli, ground spices and garlic for about 2 minutes.

4
Add all the remaining ingredients and simmer for about 3 minutes. Serve the fish with the sauce served alongside.

Serving suggestion
Serve with plain boiled rice, a cucumber relish and a mixed salad.

Variations
Substitute a firm-fleshed fish, such as haddock or monkfish, for the plaice. Use sesame seeds in place of coconut.

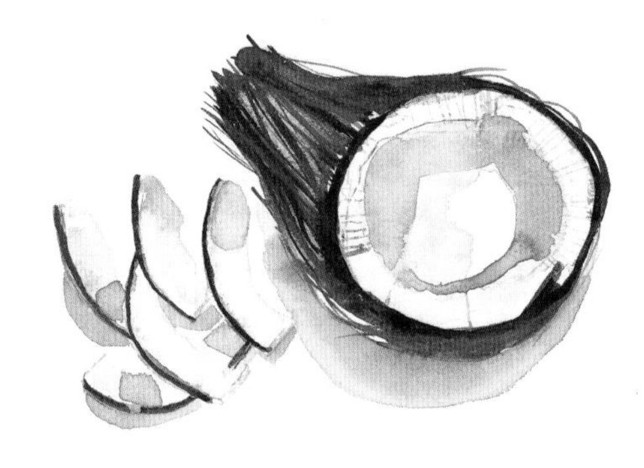

Stir-Fried Seafood

A fragrant, fiery and speedy way of serving mixed seafood of your choice.

Preparation time: 10 minutes • Cooking time: 5-6 minutes • Serves: 4

Ingredients

5 ml (1 tsp) black peppercorns

1 shallot, chopped

2 small red chillies, sliced

3 cloves garlic, crushed

30 ml (2 tbsp) vegetable oil

225 g (8 oz) shelled raw prawns

350 g (12 oz) prepared mixed seafood, e.g. clams, squid, scallops, etc.

15 ml (1 tbsp) fish sauce

15 ml (1 tbsp) lime juice

4 spring onions, sliced

Method

1
Crush the black peppercorns with a pestle and mortar. Add the shallot, chillies and garlic and continue to pound until well combined.

2
Heat the oil in a wok, add the chilli mixture and stir-fry for 1 minute.

3
Add the prawns and the other prepared seafood and stir-fry for 3-4 minutes, or until cooked through.

4
Sprinkle with the fish sauce and lime juice. Serve hot scattered with spring onion slices.

Serving suggestion
Serve with boiled egg or rice noodles and a mixed leaf salad.

Variations
Use diced raw salmon or tuna in place of prawns. Use lemon juice in place of lime juice.

Cook's tip
Prepared mixed fresh or frozen seafood is available from some supermarkets.

Steamed Fish

Steaming fish preserves its delicate flavour. The accompanying ingredients added immediately after cooking give this dish its distinct Oriental flavour.

Preparation time: 15 minutes • Cooking time: 10 minutes • Serves: 4

Ingredients

450 g (1 lb) white fish fillets, skinned

2 shallots, sliced

1 stem lemon grass, sliced

45 ml (3 tbsp) lime juice

30 ml (2 tbsp) fish sauce

5 ml (1 tsp) palm sugar

2 cloves garlic, chopped

1 red chilli, chopped

1 green chilli, chopped

Method

1
Cut the fish into thick strips and place over a saucepan of boiling water in a serving dish that will fit into the top of a steamer.

2
Scatter the sliced shallots and lemon grass over the fish and steam for 10 minutes, or until the fish is cooked through.

3
Meanwhile, combine the lime juice, fish sauce and sugar in a small bowl and stir until the sugar dissolves. Set aside.

4
Combine the garlic and chillies in another small bowl and set aside.

5
As soon as the fish is cooked, remove from the steamer and pour the fish sauce mixture over.

6
Scatter the garlic and chilli mixture over the top and serve immediately.

Serving suggestion
Serve with stir-fried vegetables and boiled rice.

Variation
Use salmon in place of white fish.

Cook's tip
Remove the seeds from the chillies for a milder-flavoured dish.

Prawn and Tamarind

Tamarind has an exotic sweet-sour taste which goes very well with prawns and combines perfectly with the spices and fresh chilli pepper in this sauce.

Preparation time: 20 minutes • Cooking time: 7 minutes • Serves: 4

Ingredients

900 g (2 lb) king prawns
30 ml (2 tbsp) vegetable oil
4 shallots, finely chopped
15 ml (1 tbsp) ground coriander
4 crushed cardamoms
10 ml (2 tsp) turmeric
A pinch of ground nutmeg
1 green chilli, seeded and thinly sliced
1 pimento, thinly sliced
Juice of 1 lime
15 ml (1 tbsp) sugar
15 ml (1 tbsp) tamarind juice
175 ml (6 fl oz) plain yogurt
Salt and freshly ground black pepper

Method

1
Shell and devein the prawns and set aside.

2
Heat the oil in a wok or large frying pan. Add the shallots and stir-fry for 1-2 minutes.

3
Add the spices and prawns and stir-fry for about 1-2 minutes.

4
Add the chilli, pimento, lime juice, sugar and tamarind and stir-fry for 2-3 minutes. Remove from the heat.

5
Stir in the yogurt and salt and pepper and serve.

Serving suggestion

Serve with cooked rice and with an accompaniment of cucumber and yogurt combined with chopped mint.

Variations

Use 1 onion in place of the shallots. Use crème fraîche in place of yogurt.

Cook's tip

Tamarind pulp is available in blocks from Oriental food stores and the juice is extracted for use in recipes. To extract the juice, use 1 part tamarind to 2 parts water. Soak the pulp in warm water for about 20-30 minutes, mashing occasionally against the side of the bowl. Strain through a sieve, pushing the juice out of the pulp with a spoon. Scrape the underside of the sieve and add to the liquid. Tamarind extract is best used the same day.

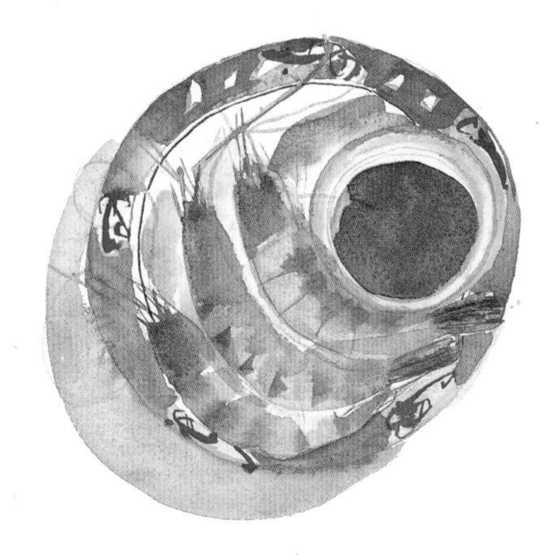

Mussels in Chilli Sauce

This hot dish employs the authentic Thai flavours of ginger, lemon grass and kaffir lime leaves.

Preparation time: 10 minutes • Cooking time: 10-12 minutes • Serves: 4

Ingredients

900 g (2 lb) live mussels

1 stem lemon grass, chopped

2.5-cm (1-in) piece root ginger, peeled and sliced

4 dried kaffir lime leaves

Fresh basil leaves and chilli flowers *(see 'Cook's tip', page 10)**, to garnish*

For the chilli sauce

3 large red chillies, chopped

15 ml (1 tbsp) chopped fresh coriander

2 cloves garlic, crushed

30 ml (2 tbsp) sunflower oil

30 ml (2 tbsp) fish sauce

15 ml (1 tbsp) sugar

15 ml (1 tbsp) fresh basil, chopped

10 ml (2 tsp) cornflour mixed with a little water

Method

1
Scrub the mussels and remove the beards, discarding any mussels with broken shells or those that do not close when tapped.

2
Bring 300 ml (½ pint) water to the boil in a saucepan or wok and add the lemon grass, ginger and lime leaves. Add the mussels, cover and boil for 5-6 minutes, or until the mussels open.

3
Drain, reserving 150 ml (¼ pint) of the cooking liquid. Discard any mussels that have not opened.

4
While the mussels are cooking, start to prepare the sauce. Using a pestle and mortar, pound the chillies, coriander and garlic together.

5
Heat the oil in a wok and fry the chilli mixture for a few minutes, then stir in the fish sauce, sugar and basil.

6
Add the reserved cooking liquid from the mussels and the cornflour mixture. Cook until slightly thickened.

7
Serve the mussels with the sauce poured over. Garnish with basil leaves and chilli flowers.

Serving suggestion

Serve with boiled noodles or rice.

Variations

Use parsley in place of basil. Use cockles in place of mussels.

Cook's tip

Kaffir lime leaves are shiny and dark and have a distinctive figure-of-eight shape. Used in a similar way to bay leaves, they can be added whole or torn in half to infuse flavour to a dish, or shredded for a garnish. They are available fresh, frozen or dried from Oriental food stores. Shredded lime zest can be substituted.

Beef in Oyster Sauce

This is a very quick dish – a stir-fry of strips of tender beef steak and Oriental-style vegetables.

Preparation time: 10 minutes • Cooking time: 10 minutes • Serves: 4

Ingredients

450 g (1 lb) sirloin steak
30 ml (2 tbsp) vegetable oil
1.25 ml (1/4 tsp) ground cumin
1.25 ml (1/4 tsp) ground coriander
175 g (6 oz) baby corn cobs
115 g (4 oz) canned bamboo shoots, drained
175 g (6 oz) mangetout
30 ml (2 tbsp) oyster sauce
10 ml (2 tsp) dark muscovado sugar
150 ml (1/4 pint) beef stock
5 ml (1 tsp) cornflour
15 ml (1 tbsp) fish sauce
Spring onion slices, to garnish

Method

1
Using a sharp knife, cut the beef into thin slices, then into strips. Set aside.

2
Heat the oil in a wok and stir-fry the beef over a high heat for about 5 minutes, or until cooked through. Stir in the ground spices and stir-fry for 1 minute.

3
Add all the vegetables, then stir in the oyster sauce, sugar and stock and bring to the boil, stirring.

4
Mix the cornflour with the fish sauce and stir into the pan, cooking until the sauce thickens. Sprinkle with slices of spring onion to garnish and serve.

Serving suggestion
Serve with boiled egg or rice noodles and steamed fresh vegetables such as broccoli florets and baby carrots.

Variations
Use pork or lamb in place of beef. Use sugar-snap peas in place of mangetout.

Cook's tip
Partially freezing the beef will make it easier to cut. Slice the meat into strips across the grain to keep it tender during cooking.

Diced Chicken and Peppers

A slightly chilli-hot stir-fry, full of interesting texture and flavour.

Preparation time: 20 minutes • Cooking time: 8 minutes • Serves: 4

Ingredients

30 ml (2 tbsp) vegetable oil

1 clove garlic, crushed

450 g (1 lb) chicken meat, skinned, boned and cut into small dice

1 small red chilli, seeded and diced

5 ml (1 tsp) cornflour

30 ml (2 tbsp) white wine

30 ml (2 tbsp) soy sauce

60 ml (4 tbsp) chicken stock

2 green peppers, sliced

A pinch of sugar (optional)

Salt

½ small can bamboo shoots, drained and diced

Method

1
Heat the oil in a wok or large frying. Add the garlic and cook for 20 seconds, then add the chicken and stir-fry until well coloured all over.

2
Add the chilli, cornflour, wine, soy sauce and stock and stir-fry for 2-3 minutes.

3
Add the peppers, sugar, if using, and salt if needed and stir-fry for 1 minute.

4
Add the bamboo shoots and stir-fry for 1-2 minutes before serving.

Serving suggestion

Accompany the dish with plain boiled rice, fried rice or Chinese noodles.

Variations

Use turkey, pork or lamb in place of chicken. Use red peppers in place of green peppers.

Cook's tip

When cooking stir-fries, make sure you have all the ingredients prepared and to hand before beginning to cook.

Mussaman Curry

An Indian-influenced Thai-style curry of beef and potatoes.

Preparation time: 25 minutes • Cooking time: 1 hour • Serves: 4

Ingredients

- *4 cardamoms*
- *2.5 ml (1/2 tsp) coriander seeds*
- *2.5 ml (1/2 tsp) caraway seeds*
- *2 whole cloves*
- *5 small red chillies, chopped*
- *1 clove garlic, crushed*
- *1 stem lemon grass, roughly chopped*
- *2 spring onions, chopped*
- *1.25 ml (1/4 tsp) root ginger*
- *1.25 ml (1/4 tsp) ground nutmeg*
- *15 ml (1 tbsp) sunflower oil*
- *Vegetable oil, for shallow frying*
- *350 g (12 oz) potatoes, peeled and cut into chunks*
- *2-3 onions, peeled and cut into wedges*
- *675 g (1 1/2 lb) sirloin steak, cut into bite-sized chunks*
- *425 ml (1 3/4 pints) thin coconut milk (see 'Cook's tip')*
- *30 ml (2 tbsp) dark muscovado sugar*
- *5 ml (1 tsp) tamarind juice (see 'Cook's tip', page 32)*
- *Chopped fresh coriander, to garnish*

Method

1
Crush the cardamoms with the side of a knife and remove the seeds.

2
Place the coriander, caraway and cardamom seeds and cloves in a wok and dry-fry for 1 minute, tossing frequently to prevent burning. Remove from the heat.

3
Mix the fried seeds, chillies, garlic, lemon grass, spring onions, ginger, nutmeg and sunflower oil together and pound with a pestle and mortar.

4
Heat the vegetable oil for shallow frying in a wok and fry the potatoes and onions for 5 minutes, or until they begin to soften. Remove using a slotted spoon, place on a plate and set aside.

5
Add the meat to the pan and fry until browned. Stir in a quarter of the coconut milk and simmer gently for about 30 minutes, or until the meat is very tender, stirring occasionally.

6
Remove the meat from the wok with a slotted spoon and set aside. Add the chilli mixture to the wok and boil rapidly for 5 minutes, then blend in the remaining coconut milk.

7
Return the meat, potatoes and onions to the wok. Stir in the sugar and tamarind juice and cook gently for 20 minutes, stirring occasionally. Garnish with chopped coriander and serve.

Serving suggestion

Serve with boiled brown or white and wild rice and prawn crackers.

Variations

Use lamb or pork in place of beef. Use sweet potatoes in place of standard potatoes.

Cook's tip

Coconut milk is available in cans from Oriental food stores and many supermarkets. It separates in the can into layers – the cream is very thick and can be scooped to leave the thin milk underneath, which is the correct consistency for this recipe. For thick coconut milk, stir together the complete contents of the can.

Kung Pao Lamb

This memorable dish, with its unusual blend of flavours, is named after a past governor of Sichuan, whose official title was 'Kung Pao'.

Preparation time: 20 minutes • Cooking time: 10 minutes • Serves: 4

Ingredients

30 ml (2 tbsp) vegetable oil
450 g (1 lb) lamb fillet or meat from the leg, thinly sliced
1 clove garlic, finely chopped
1 small piece fresh ginger root, peeled and grated
½ red chilli, seeded and finely chopped
60 ml (4 tbsp) soy sauce
125 ml (4 fl oz) lamb or vegetable stock
30 ml (2 tbsp) white wine
5 ml (1 tsp) vinegar
5 ml (1 tsp) sugar
15 ml (1 tbsp) cornflour
1 small red pepper, seeded and cut into small dice
1 small green pepper, seeded and cut into small dice
A dash of sesame oil
4 spring onions, sliced
55 g (2 oz) roasted peanuts

Method

1
Heat the oil in a wok or large frying pan. Add the lamb and stir-fry until coloured all over.

2
Add the garlic, ginger and chilli and stir-fry for a further 1-2 minutes.

3
Mix the soy sauce, stock, wine, vinegar, sugar and cornflour together and add to the meat.

4
Cook over a medium heat for a further 4-6 minutes, or until the lamb is tender, stirring occasionally.

5
Add the diced peppers, sesame oil, spring onions and peanuts and stir-fry for 1-2 minutes. Serve immediately.

Serving suggestion
Serve with plain boiled rice or fried rice.

Variations
Use pork or beef in place of lamb. Use cashew nuts or almonds in place of the peanuts.

Steamed Pork Cups

Served with a light salad and accompanied by a hot dipping sauce, this spicy pork mixture makes an ideal lunchtime dish.

Preparation time: 20 minutes • Cooking time: 20 minutes • Serves: 4-6

Ingredients

450 g (1 lb) lean pork
5 cloves garlic, crushed
6 spring onions, sliced
2 green chillies, sliced
15 ml (1 tbsp) roasted cashew nuts
5 ml (1 tsp) shrimp paste
30 ml (2 tbsp) soy sauce
15 ml (1 tbsp) fresh coriander leaves and stems
A pinch of white pepper
5 ml (1 tsp) palm sugar
125 ml (4 fl oz) thick coconut milk
(see 'Cook's tip', page 40)
2 egg whites

For the salad

1 red pepper, seeded and sliced
1 green pepper, seeded sliced
115 g (4 oz) bean sprouts
30 ml (2 tbsp) lime juice
15 ml (1 tbsp) fish sauce

Method

1
Cut the pork into chunks, place in a food processor and process briefly.

2
Add the garlic, spring onions, chillies, cashew nuts, shrimp paste, soy sauce, coriander, pepper and sugar to the processor and process again until all the ingredients are chopped and well combined.

3
Transfer the pork mixture to a bowl and beat in the coconut milk. Whisk the egg whites until standing in soft peaks, then fold into the mixture. Pile the pork mixture into 4 or 6 small dishes or ramekins.

4
Place in steamer and steam for 20 minutes, or until the mixture is set and cooked through, then remove from the steamer and allow to cool.

5
To make the salad, combine the peppers and bean sprouts in a bowl and sprinkle with the lime juice and fish sauce.

6
Turn the pork out of the dishes and cut into wedges. Serve with the pepper and bean sprout salad and a hot dipping sauce of your choice.

Serving suggestion

Serve with a mixed leaf salad.

Variations

Use chicken or beef in place of pork. Use peanuts in place of cashew nuts.

Cook's tips

Place a sheet of greaseproof paper or foil over the pork as it cooks, to prevent condensation dripping into the dishes. Shrimp paste is available in small jars from Oriental food stores. It has a very pungent smell, so should be kept in an airtight glass jar. It should always be fried before using.

Beef and Leek Skewers

An unusual combination of ingredients, these kebabs are nutritious as well as delicious.

Preparation time: 15 minutes, plus 30 minutes standing time • Cooking time: 10 minutes • Serves: 4

Ingredients

60 ml (4 tbsp) caster sugar

30 ml (2 tbsp) tamarind juice
(see 'Cook's tip', page 32)

15 ml (1 tbsp) grated root ginger

150 ml (1/2 pint) light soy sauce

Freshly ground black pepper

450 g (1 lb) rump steak

4 leeks

45 ml (3 tbsp) vegetable oil

Fresh herb sprigs, to garnish

Method

1
In a large bowl, mix together the sugar, tamarind juice, ginger, soy sauce and pepper.

2
Cut the steak into 2.5-cm (1-in) cubes. Trim the leeks to leave only the white and pale green parts, then cut into 2.5-cm (1-in) pieces.

3
Place the beef and leeks in the marinade mixture and mix together thoroughly to coat evenly. Set aside for 30 minutes.

4
Thread the beef and leeks alternately onto thin wooden kebab skewers.

5
Heat the oil in a large shallow frying pan. Cook the kebabs in the oil, turning frequently to prevent them burning.

6
Add the marinade mixture to the pan and cook quickly until it has reduced to a thick syrupy consistency.

7
Coat the kebabs with the marinade syrup before serving. Garnish with fresh herb sprigs and serve.

Serving suggestion

Serve with boiled rice and a mixed salad.

Variations

Use chicken or turkey breast in place of beef. Use small onions or shallots, halved, in place of the leeks.

Cook's tip

If tamarind pulp (see 'Cook's tip', page 32) is not available, substitute 30 ml (2 tbsp) lemon juice.

Beef and Mangetout Stir-Fry

A quick and easy stir-fry for a flavourful after-work meal.

Preparation time: 20 minutes • Cooking time: 15 minutes • Serves: 4

Ingredients

400 g (14 oz) lean beef steak

75 ml (5 tbsp) vegetable oil

Salt and freshly ground black pepper

3 onions, finely chopped

400 g (14 oz) mangetout

2 sprigs of fresh basil, chopped

175 ml (6 fl oz) beef stock

2 beefsteak tomatoes, weighing about 400 g (14 oz) in total, skinned, seeded and sliced

45 ml (3 tbsp) soy sauce

Chopped fresh basil leaves, to garnish

Method

1
Slice the beef into thin strips. Heat the oil in a wok or large frying pan, add the beef and stir-fry for about 3 minutes. Season the meat to taste with salt and pepper, remove from the pan, place on a plate and keep hot.

2
Add the onions to the wok and stir-fry until softened.

3
Add the mangetout, basil and stock, cover the pan and cook for about 3 minutes, stirring once or twice.

4
Add the tomatoes and cook for a further 3 minutes.

5
Return the beef to the wok and stir in the soy sauce. Adjust the seasoning, then heat until hot.

6
Sprinkle over the chopped fresh basil to garnish and serve immediately.

Serving suggestion

Serve with boiled egg noodles.

Variations

Use pork or lamb in place of beef. Use sugar-snap peas or baby corn cobs in place of mangetout. Use parsley in place of the basil.

Beef with Pineapple and Peppers

A delicious and colourful combination of ingredients with classic Oriental sweet and sour flavours.

Preparation time: 30 minutes • Cooking time: 10 minutes • Serves 4

Ingredients

450 g (1 lb) fillet or rump steak
1 small pineapple
1 green pepper
1 red pepper
15 ml (1 tbsp) peanut oil
1 onion, peeled and roughly chopped
2 cloves garlic, crushed
2.5-cm (1-in) piece root ginger, peeled and thinly sliced
5 ml (1 tsp) sesame oil
30 ml (2 tbsp) light soy sauce
15 ml (1 tbsp) dark soy suae
5 ml (1 tsp) sugar
15 ml (1 tbsp) brown sauce
Salt and freshly ground black pepper

Method

1
Using a sharp knife, cut the steak into thin strips.

2
Carefully peel the pineapple and cut out any eyes using a sharp knife or potato peeler. Cut the pineapple into slices, then chop into bite-sized pieces, removing the hard core.

3
Slice the peppers in half. Remove and discard the cores and seeds. Chop the pepper flesh into thin strips.

4
Heat the peanut oil in a wok or large frying pan and gently fry the onion, garlic and ginger, stirring continuously, until the onion has softened slightly.

5
Add the strips of beef and the strips of pepper, and continue stir-frying for 3 minutes.

6
Add the pineapple and stir-fry for 2 minutes.

7
Remove the meat, vegetables and fruit from the wok with a slotted spoon, place on a plate and set aside.

8
Stir the sesame oil into the juices in the wok and add the soy sauces, sugar, brown sauce and 60 ml (4 tbsp) water. Simmer rapidly for 30 seconds to reduce and thicken the sauce.

9
Return the fruit, vegetables and meat to the wok. Season and heat through, stirring. Serve immediately.

Serving suggestion
Serve with spring rolls and boiled rice.

Variations
Use lean pork in place of the beef. Use papaya or mango in place of the pineapple.

Curried Chicken Kebabs

This is a spicy yet fragrant dish, served with a cooling accompaniment of cucumber and yogurt.

Preparation time: 10 minutes, plus 1 hour marinating time • Cooking time: 10-15 minutes • Serves: 4

Ingredients

3 skinless, boneless chicken breasts
Lime slices, to garnish
Juice and finely grated rind of 1 lime
Salt and freshly ground black pepper

For the marinade

30 ml (2 tbsp) vegetable oil
1 clove garlic, crushed
10 ml (2 tsp) curry powder
1.25 ml (1/4 tsp) cayenne pepper
15 ml (1 tbsp) chopped fresh coriander leaves

For the sauce

1/2 cucumber, grated
300 ml (1/2 pint) plain yogurt
15 ml (1 tbsp) chopped fresh mint
5 ml (1 tsp) mango chutney
A pinch of salt and pepper

Method

1
Cut the chicken into 2.5-cm (1-in) cubes. Combine the ingredients for the marinade and mix with the chicken to coat each piece all over. Leave to marinate for 1 hour.

2
Thread the chicken onto 4 skewers and place on a grill rack. Grill under a medium heat for 10-15 minutes, until cooked and tender, turning frequently and basting in the marinade.

3
While the chicken is marinating, make the sauce. Sprinkle the grated cucumber lightly with salt and leave to stand for 30 minutes.

4
Rinse thoroughly and pat dry with absorbent kitchen paper. Combine with the remaining sauce ingredients and serve with the hot kebabs. Garnish with lime slices.

Serving suggestion

Serve on a bed of boiled herb- or saffron-flavoured rice.

Variations

Use turkey or pork in place of chicken. Other herbs or spices can be added to the marinade. Omit the cayenne pepper for a milder flavour.

Japanese Steamer

The Japanese are renowned for their elegant cuisine, and this recipe is no exception.

Preparation time: 20 minutes, plus soaking and standing times • Cooking time: 20 minutes (microwave on HIGH) • Serves: 4

Ingredients

115 g (4 oz) buckwheat noodles

A pinch of salt

16 dried black mushrooms, soaked overnight

115 g (4 oz) small button mushrooms

8 baby corn cobs

1 small piece ginger root, peeled and finely grated

150 ml (1/4 pint) soy sauce

60 ml (4 tbsp) vegetable stock

15 ml (1 tbsp) sherry

5 ml (1 tsp) cornflour

1 packet dried sea spinach, soaked for 1 hour

3 packets tofu (bean curd), drained

1 small daikon (mooli) radish, sliced

1 small bunch fresh chives

1 lemon, thinly sliced

Method

1
Carefully arrange the noodles in a bowl containing 600 ml (1 pint) boiling water and add salt.

2
Cover the bowl with cling film and pierce several times with the tip of a sharp knife. Cook the noodles in a microwave oven on HIGH for 6 minutes. Leave the noodles to stand, still covered, for 10 minutes.

3
Remove the stems from the black mushrooms and discard.

4
Return the mushroom caps to the soaking liquor and heat in the microwave on HIGH for 5 minutes. Set aside until required.

5
Place the button mushrooms and the baby corn cobs into a small bowl with 15 ml (1 tbsp) water. Cover the bowl with cling film and puncture as before. Cook for 2 minutes on HIGH and set aside.

6
Place the ginger, soy sauce, stock, sherry and cornflour into a small bowl and whisk until the cornflour is blended.

7
Cook the sauce on HIGH for 3 minutes, or until it has thickened and cleared.

8
Drain the sea spinach, mushrooms and noodles.

9
Slice the tofu into 1-cm (½-in) slices with a sharp knife.

10
Arrange all the prepared ingredients on 4 separate serving dishes and pour a little of the sauce over.

11
Heat each dish on HIGH for 1 minute, then garnish with the radish, chives and lemon slices. Serve with the remaining sauce alongside.

Serving suggestion

Serve with a mixed leaf salad or a green salad.

Variations

Use egg noodles in place of buckwheat noodles. Use garlic in place of ginger.

Sweet-and-Sour Nuggets

Serve these crunchy almond nuggets with boiled or egg-fried rice.

Preparation time: 30 minutes, plus chilling time • Cooking time: 20-25 minutes (microwave on HIGH) • Serves: 4

Ingredients

25 g (1 oz) vegetable margarine

1 shallot, peeled and finely chopped

25 g (1 oz) plain flour

150 ml (1/4 pint) milk

55 g (2 oz) ground almonds

55 g (2 oz) water chestnuts, finely chopped

5 ml (1 tsp) chopped fresh parsley

5 ml (1 tsp) ground ginger

1 egg, beaten

Salt and freshly ground black pepper

Dry breadcrumbs, for coating

Sesame seeds, for coating

60 ml (4 tbsp) groundnut oil, for frying

55 g (2 oz) soft brown sugar

60 ml (4 tbsp) vinegar

30 ml (2 tbsp) tomato ketchup

30 ml (2 tbsp) soy sauce

225-g (8-oz) can pineapple chunks

25 g (1 oz) cornflour

1 green pepper, seeded and sliced

2 spring onions, trimmed and cut into thin diagonal slices

1 small can bamboo shoots, drained

225 g (8 oz) fresh bean sprouts

Method

1

Place the margarine in a large bowl in a microwave oven and cook on HIGH for 1 minute, to melt.

2

Add the shallot and stir well to coat evenly. Cook for 30 seconds on HIGH to soften. Stir the flour into the shallot mixture, blending it well with a wooden spoon to form a paste. Gradually add the milk, beating well and cooking for 30 seconds between additions, until the sauce is thick and smooth. Stir the almonds, water chestnuts, parsley, ginger, half the beaten egg and some seasoning into the shallot sauce, mixing well to form a firm paste.

3

Place the almond paste in a dish and chill in a refrigerator until firm. Divide the chilled mixture into 16 evenly sized balls.

4

Place the breadcrumbs and the sesame seeds into a dish and mix together thoroughly. Brush each almond nugget with the remaining beaten egg, then coat in the breadcrumbs and sesame seed mixture.

5

Heat a browning dish on HIGH for 5 minutes. Add the oil and fry the coated nuggets for 3-4 minutes, stirring frequently to brown evenly. Drain the nuggets on absorbent kitchen paper and keep warm while preparing the sauce.

6

Mix together the sugar, vinegar, ketchup and soy sauce in a deep-sided bowl or jug. Drain the juice from the pineapple and stir into the vinegar mixture. Reserve the pineapple chunks. Blend the cornflour into the sauce liquid, whisking until it is smooth. Cook the sauce on HIGH for 2-3 minutes.

7

Add the peppers, onions and bamboo shoots to the sauce. Chop the pineapple chunks into small pieces and stir into the sauce, mixing all the ingredients together thoroughly. Heat the sauce through for 1 minute.

8

Arrange the bean sprouts on a serving dish and place the nuggets on top. Heat through for 1 minute. Pour a little of the sauce over the nuggets and serving any remaining sauce separately.

Chinese Black Bean Casserole

Black beans are a traditional Chinese delicacy, and impart a rich flavour to a variety of dishes. They are available from Oriental food stores.

Preparation time: 20 minutes, plus standing time • Cooking time: 1 hour 35 minutes (microwave) • Serves: 4

Ingredients

450 g (1 lb) Chinese black beans, soaked overnight
1 small piece root ginger, grated
1 piece star anise
1 clove garlic, crushed
10 ml (2 tsp) five-spice powder
6-8 sticks celery
90 ml (3 fl oz) sherry
15 ml (1 tbsp) soy sauce
5 ml (1 tsp) sesame seed oil
1 small can water chestnuts
115 g (4 oz) bean sprouts
4 spring onions, shredded

Method

1
Drain the beans and place in a large bowl. Add the ginger, star anise, garlic and five-spice powder. Pour over enough cold water to just cover the beans.

2
Cover the bowl with cling film and pierce several times with the tip of a sharp knife. Cook the beans in a microwave oven on HIGH for 10 minutes, then reduce the power setting to MEDIUM and continue cooking for a further 1 hour, or until the beans are completely soft, stirring once or twice.

3
Cut the celery into thin slices and add to the beans. Re-cover the bowl and cook for a further 15 minutes on HIGH, stirring occasionally.

4
Stir the sherry, soy sauce and oil into the beans and celery and cook for a further 5 minutes, uncovered, on HIGH. If after this time a lot of cooking liquid remains, continue cooking on HIGH, stirring occasionally, until most of the liquid has been absorbed.

5
Drain the water chestnuts. Using a sharp knife, slice each water chestnut into thin diagonal slices and add to the bean casserole. Stir well and heat through for 1 minute on HIGH.

6
Mix together the bean sprouts and spring onions and sprinkle over the top of the casserole just before serving.

Serving suggestion

Serve with vegetable fried rice or boiled brown rice.

Variations

Use bamboo shoots in place of water chestnuts. Use unsweetened apple juice in place of sherry.

Sweet-and-Sour Peanuts

This highly nutritious meal is speedy and simple to prepare, as well as satisfying in texture and flavour.

Preparation time: 15 minutes • Cooking time: 10 minutes • Serves: 4

Ingredients

85 g (3 oz) muscovado sugar
75 ml (5 tbsp) wine vinegar
45 ml (3 tbsp) soy sauce
15 ml (1 tbsp) arrowroot
1 large red pepper
115 g (4 oz) fresh bean sprouts
115 g (4 oz) shelled, unsalted roasted peanuts
225 g (8 oz) canned bamboo shoots, drained

Method

1
Place the sugar, wine vinegar and soy sauce in a saucepan. Add the arrowroot and stir until well blended.

2
Bring to the boil, stirring, and cook until the mixture has thickened and cleared. Set aside.

3
Halve the pepper and remove the seeds and discard. Using a sharp knife, cut the flesh into thin strips about 1 x 5 cm (½ x 2 in).

4
Stir the pepper strips and all the remaining ingredients into the thickened sauce mixture.

5
Bring to the boil, then reduce the heat and simmer until the pepper strips are tender, stirring occasionally. Serve.

Serving suggestion

Serve with boiled brown or white rice, or a mixture of both.

Variations

Use cashew nuts in place of peanuts. Add 55 g (2 oz) fresh chopped pineapple. Use sliced, canned water chestnuts in place of bamboo shoots.

Nasi Goreng

This is an interpretation of the classic Indonesian dish which combines rice with lean pork and flavourings.

Preparation time: 20 minutes • Cooking time: 15 minutes • Serves: 4

Ingredients

200 g (7 oz) long-grain rice

Salt

75 ml (5 tbsp) olive oil

3 onions, finely chopped

1 clove garlic, finely chopped

400 g (14 oz) lean pork, cut into small cubes or thin strips

30-60 ml (2-4 tbsp) soy sauce

Tabasco sauce, to taste

1 small Iceberg lettuce

1 spring onion

Method

1
Cook the rice in a large saucepan of lightly salted water for about 15 minutes, or until tender. Drain thoroughly and keep hot.

2
Meanwhile, heat the oil in a pan, then add the onions and garlic and cook until softened. Remove from the pan using a slotted spoon, place on a plate and keep hot.

3
Add the pork and cook until browned all over, stirring frequently.

4
Add the rice and soy sauce and cook for 1 minute, stirring.

5
Add the onion and garlic and season to taste with salt and Tabasco.

6
Wash and dry the lettuce and separate into leaves. Wash the spring onion and slice into small rings. Serve the pork mixture on a bed of lettuce leaves and garnish with the spring onion rings.

Serving suggestion

Serve with stir-fried mixed vegetables such as bean sprouts, carrots and courgettes.

Variations

Use lamb or beef in place of pork. Use brown rice in place of white rice – allow about 30-35 minutes boiling time for brown rice.

Cook's tip

Classically, this dish is prepared using sambal oelek (Oriental chilli sauce) rather than Tabasco sauce. Sambal oelek is available from Oriental food stores.

Ham and Bean Fried Rice

This makes an interesting side dish for a complete Oriental meal or a light main course on its own.

Preparation time: 15 minutes • Cooking time: 10 minutes • Serves: 4

Ingredients

45 ml (3 tbsp) vegetable oil

2 eggs, beaten

115 g (4 oz) ham, chopped

225 g (8 oz) rice, cooked

115 g (4 oz) French beans, cut into thin diagonal slices

15 ml (1 tbsp) soy sauce

4 spring onions, chopped

Spring onion brushes *(see 'Cook's tip', page 10)**, to garnish*

Method

1

Heat half the oil in a frying pan. Add half the beaten egg and cook until set, then turn over and cook the other side. Remove from the pan and keep hot. Repeat with the remaining egg.

2

Heat the remaining oil in the frying pan. Add the ham and rice and cook for 5 minutes, stirring occasionally.

3

Add the beans, soy sauce and spring onions, mix well and cook for 2 minutes.

4

Slice the cooked eggs into thin strips and scatter over the top of the rice. Serve, garnished with spring onion brushes.

Serving suggestion

Serve with thick slices of fresh crusty bread.

Variations

Use smoked ham in place of unsmoked ham. Use mangetout in place of French beans.

Cook's tip

Once the egg strips have been cooked, they can be kept warm but will toughen if reheated. Snip them into strips using a clean pair of kitchen scissors.

Baked Pineapple Rice

This unusual and attractive rice dish originates from Bangkok and the central plains of Thailand.

Preparation time: 20 minutes • Cooking time: 25 minutes • Serves: 6

Ingredients

For the Yellow Curry Paste (makes 75-90 ml/5-6 tbsp)

30 ml (2 tbsp) cumin seeds

30 ml (2 tbsp) coriander seeds

3 stems lemon grass, chopped

15 ml (1 tbsp) grated root ginger

6 red chillies, seeded and chopped

5 ml (1 tsp) salt

3 cloves garlic, crushed

1 small shallot, finely chopped

5 ml (1 tsp) ground turmeric

5 ml (1 tsp) shrimp paste

1 pineapple

30 ml (2 tbsp) vegetable oil

1 clove garlic, chopped

4 shallots, chopped

15 ml (1 tbsp) Yellow Curry Paste

450 g (1 lb) cooked rice

150 ml (1/4 pint) thick coconut milk
(see 'Cook's tip', page 40)

55 g (2 oz) raisins

55 g (2 oz) toasted cashew nuts

Chilli flowers *(see 'Cook's tip', page 10)**, to garnish*

Method

1
To make the Yellow Curry Paste, place the seeds in a wok without any oil and dry-fry for 3-4 minutes, shaking the wok frequently to prevent the spices from burning. Remove from the heat and set aside.

2
Using a large pestle and mortar, pound the lemon grass and ginger until well crushed. Add the chillies and salt and continue pounding for about 4 minutes.

3
Add the garlic and shallot and pound until broken down, then add the fried spices and turmeric. Add the shrimp paste and continue to pound until a smooth paste is formed.

4
Cut the pineapple in half lengthways, keeping the leaves attached. Scoop out the flesh using a tablespoon and a paring knife, to leave two shells with a thin border of flesh attached. Chop half the flesh to use later in the dish; the remaining pineapple is not needed.

5
Heat the oil in a wok or large frying pan and stir-fry the garlic and shallots until softened. Stir in the curry paste and stir-fry for 1 minute.

6
Remove the pan from the heat, add the rice and toss together with the shallot mixture. Stir in the coconut milk, raisins, chopped pineapple and cashew nuts, mixing well.

7
Pile the rice mixture into the pineapple shells. Wrap the pineapple leaves in foil to prevent them from burning and place on a baking sheet.

8
Bake in a preheated oven at 170°C/325°F/Gas Mark 3 for 20 minutes. Remove from the foil and serve garnished with chilli flowers.

Serving suggestion

Serve with a mixed dark leaf salad.

Variations

Use walnuts or peanuts in place of cashew nuts. Use chopped ready-to-eat dried apricots or sultanas in place of raisins.

Spicy Steamed Pork with Noodles

Serve this tasty noodle dish as part of a complete Oriental meal or on its own for a substantial snack or light lunch.

Preparation time: 20 minutes • Cooking time: 20 minutes • Serves: 4

Ingredients

For the Red Curry Paste (makes 45-60 ml/3-4 tbsp)

12 small red chillies, chopped

3 cloves garlic, crushed

1 stem lemon grass, chopped

1 small onion, finely chopped

5 ml (1 tsp) grated root ginger

10 ml (2 tsp) chopped coriander leaves and stems

A large pinch of ground cumin

5 ml (1 tsp) shrimp paste

30 ml (1 tbsp) vegetable oil

225 g (8 oz) minced pork

5 ml (1 tsp) ground coriander

5 ml (1 tsp) ground cumin

5 ml (1 tsp) ground turmeric

1 bunch bok choy or spinach, washed

15-30 ml (1-2 tbsp) Red Curry Paste

5 ml (1 tsp) shrimp paste

150 ml (1/4 pint) thick coconut milk (see 'Cook's tip', page 40)

175 g (6 oz) egg noodles

Chopped fresh coriander, to garnish

Method

1
To make the Red Curry Paste, pound the chillies, garlic, lemon grass and onion with a pestle and mortar until the mixture is well bruised and the juices begin to blend.

2
Add all the remaining ingredients except the oil and continue to pound until a paste is formed. Finally, blend in the oil.

3
Place the minced pork and ground spices in a food processor and process until very finely chopped. Shape the pork mixture into small balls using dampened hands.

4
Tear the bok choy or spinach into large pieces and place in a heatproof dish that will fit into a steamer. Arrange the meat balls on top.

5
Mix together the curry paste, shrimp paste and coconut milk and pour over the meat balls. Cover and steam for 20 minutes.

6
Meanwhile, cook the noodles as directed on the packet. Mix the noodles together with the pork and bok choy or arrange the noodles on a plate and pile the pork mixture on top. Garnish with a sprinkling of chopped coriander and serve.

Serving suggestion

Serve with a mixed, chopped salad.

Variations

Use lamb, beef or chicken in place of pork. Use chilli paste in place of curry paste.

Cook's tip

The pork can be mixed with the spices by hand. Add a little beaten egg if necessary, to help bind the mixture together.

Chaing Mai Noodles

Originally from Burma, this dish has taken on distinct Thai influences.

Preparation time: 20 minutes • Cooking time: 20 minutes • Serves: 4-6

Ingredients

30 ml (2 tbsp) vegetable oil

2 cloves garlic, crushed

4 shallots, chopped

15 ml (1 tbsp) Red Curry Paste *(page 68)*

2.5 ml (½ tsp) ground turmeric

A pinch of ground cumin

A pinch of ground coriander

300 ml (½ pint) thick coconut milk *(see 'Cook's tip', page 40)*

225 g (8 oz) rump or sirloin steak, thinly sliced

75 ml (5 tbsp) fish sauce

55 g (2 oz) palm sugar

15 ml (1 tbsp) soy sauce

30 ml (2 tbsp) lime juice

15 ml (1 tbsp) fresh chives, chopped

450 g (1 lb) fresh egg noodles

Chilli flowers *(see 'Cook's tip', page 10)* *and crispy egg noodles (optional), to garnish*

Method

1
Heat the oil in a wok and stir-fry the garlic and shallots until softened.

2
Stir in the curry paste, turmeric, cumin and coriander. Stir-fry for 1 minute.

3
Add the coconut milk and bring to the boil, reduce the heat and add the beef. Simmer for 15-20 minutes, or until the beef is cooked, stirring occasionally.

4
Stir in the fish sauce, sugar, soy sauce, lime juice and chives.

5
Meanwhile, cook the egg noodles in boiling water for 1 minute. Drain and arrange on a serving dish. Spoon the beef on top and serve garnished with chilli flowers and crispy noodles, if you like.

Serving suggestion

Serve with a mixed green leaf and tomato salad.

Variations

Use lamb or pork in place of beef. Use fresh pasta in place of egg noodles.

Cook's tips

Cut the steak across the grain to keep it tender during cooking. To make the noodle garnish, deep-fry a few of the cooked egg noodles until crispy.

Spicy Shanghai Noodle Salad

A quick and delicious salad of spicy noodles and mixed vegetables and fruit.

Preparation time: 25 minutes • Cooking time: 10 minutes • Serves: 4-6

Ingredients

115 g (4 oz) cellophane noodles
250 g (9 oz) fillet of pork
Salt and freshly ground black pepper
Curry powder, for seasoning
Plain flour, for coating
45 ml (3 tbsp) vegetable oil
280-g (10-oz) can peas
200-g (7-oz) can mandarin orange segments
175-g (6-oz) can bean sprouts
225-g (8-oz) can bamboo shoots
5-cm (2-in) piece root ginger

For the dressing

30 ml (2 tbsp) soya oil
30 ml (2 tbsp) wine vinegar
30 ml (2 tbsp) soy sauce
15-30 ml (1-2 tbsp) curry powder
Sambal oelek

Method

1
Place the noodles in a bowl, pour over boiling water and leave to soak for 3-4 minutes. Drain the noodles, rinse with cold water, then drain again thoroughly. Cut into shorter lengths with a sharp knife and set aside.

2
Slice the pork into thin strips and season with salt and pepper and curry powder, then sprinkle with flour.

3
Heat the vegetable oil in a wok or large frying pan, add the pork and stir-fry until cooked and browned all over. Remove from the pan using a slotted spoon, place on a plate and set aside to cool.

4
Drain the peas, mandarins, bean sprouts and bamboo shoots. Cut the bamboo shoots into strips and cut the ginger into thin slices. Place in a bowl with the noodles and pork and toss together to mix well.

5
For the dressing, in a small bowl mix together the oil, wine vinegar, soy sauce, curry powder and enough sambal oelek to cover the tip of a knife. Drizzle the mixture over the noodle salad, then toss to mix.

6
Set aside for about 15 minutes to allow the dressing to be absorbed into the salad before serving. Adjust the seasoning and serve.

Serving suggestion
Serve with rice crackers or thin slices of lightly toasted bread.

Variations
Use fresh pasta in place of noodles. Use canned peach or apricot slices in place of mandarins.
Use lamb, beef or turkey in place of pork.

Ten Varieties of Beauty

The ten varieties refers to the selection of vegetables in this exotic Chinese-style dish, which is simplicity itself when made using a microwave oven.

Preparation time: 30 minutes • Cooking time: 15 minutes (microwave on HIGH) • Serves: 4

Ingredients

10 Chinese dried mushrooms
2 carrots, peeled
60 ml (4 tbsp) vegetable oil
3 sticks celery, diagonally sliced
85 g (3 oz) mangetout
1 red pepper, seeded and sliced
8 baby corn cobs
4 spring onions, diagonally sliced
55 g (2 oz) fresh bean sprouts
10 water chestnuts, sliced
½ small can sliced bamboo shoots, drained
300 ml (½ pint) vegetable stock
30 ml (2 tbsp) cornflour
45 ml (3 tbsp) light soy sauce
5 ml (1 tsp) sesame oil

Method

1
Place the mushrooms in a bowl and pour over just enough boiling water to cover. Leave to stand for 20 minutes.

2
Drain the mushrooms from the water and remove and discard the tough stalks.

3
Cut the carrots into ribbons with a potato peeler, slicing the vegetables into thin strips.

4
Heat a browning dish in a microwave oven on HIGH for 5 minutes. Pour on the oil and heat for 30 seconds on HIGH.

5
Add the carrots and celery to the oil and stir well. Cook for 1 minute on HIGH. Remove the vegetables with a slotted spoon, place on a plate and set aside.

6
Add the mangetout, red pepper and corn cobs to the browning dish, stir well and cook for 1 minute on HIGH. Set aside with the carrot and celery.

7
Cook the spring onions, bean sprouts, water chestnuts and bamboo shoots in the browning dish for 1 minute on HIGH, adding the Chinese mushrooms after 30 seconds and stirring well into the other vegetables before continuing the cooking.

8
Mix all the vegetables together and set aside.

9
Place all the remaining ingredients in a jug or deep-sided bowl. Cook for 2-3 minutes on HIGH, or until the sauce has thickened and cleared, stirring once or twice.

10
Pour the sauce over the vegetables and stir carefully to avoid breaking them up.

11
Reheat the vegetables for 1-2 minutes on HIGH before serving.

Serving suggestion

Serve with boiled rice or egg noodles.

Variations

Use sugar-snap peas in place of mangetout. Use parsnips in place of carrots.

Vegetable Stir-Fry

A medley of crisp, colourful and delicious vegetables to enjoy either on their own or as an accompaniment to an Oriental main course.

Preparation time: 20 minutes • Cooking time: 10 minutes • Serves: 4

Ingredients

4 spears broccoli
115 g (4 oz) baby corn cobs
30 ml (2 tbsp) vegetable oil
1 red pepper, seeded and sliced
115 g (4 oz) mangetout, trimmed
55 g (2 oz) water chestnuts, sliced
1 clove garlic, crushed
115 g (4 oz) mushrooms, sliced
15 ml (1 tbsp) cornflour
90 ml (6 tbsp) vegetable stock
60 ml (4 tbsp) soy sauce
30 ml (2 tbsp) sherry
115 g (4 oz) bean sprouts
2 spring onions, sliced

Method

1
Cut off the broccoli florets and reserve. Slice the stalks diagonally. Slice the baby corn cobs in half lengthways.

2
Heat the oil in a wok or large frying pan. Add the broccoli stalks and baby corn cobs and stir-fry for 1-2 minutes.

3
Add the red pepper, mangetout, water chestnuts, garlic, mushrooms and the broccoli florets and stir-fry for a further 1-2 minutes.

4
Mix together the cornflour, stock, soy sauce and sherry in a small bowl, add to the wok and stir-fry for 2-3 minutes, until hot and thickened. Add the bean sprouts and spring onions and stir-fry for a further 1-2 minute, until the vegetables are cooked. Serve immediately.

Serving suggestion

Serve with boiled egg or rice noodles.

Variations

Use cauliflower in place of broccoli. Use courgettes in place of mushrooms. Use sweetened apple juice in place of the sherry.

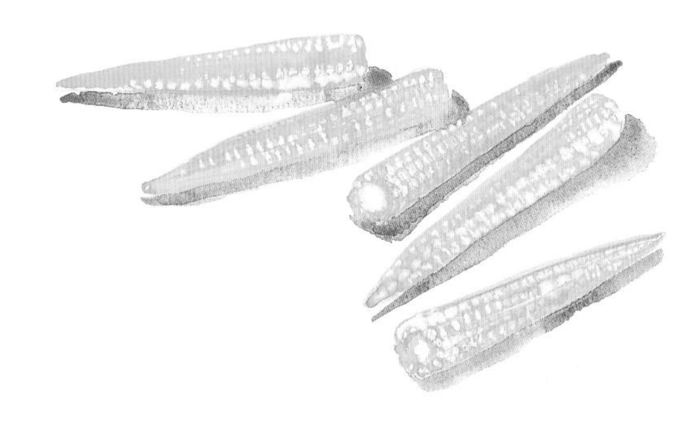

Spicy Cucumbers

This unusual dish is Chinese in origin. Brief microwave cooking helps intensify the flavours. If you don't have a microwave oven, simply omit the cooking process, thoroughly mix together all the ingredients and chill before serving.

Preparation time: 30 minutes • Cooking time: 20 minutes (microwave on HIGH) • Serves: 4

Ingredients

1 large cucumber

Salt

45 ml (3 tbsp) light soy sauce

A pinch of five-spice powder

1.25 ml (1/4 tsp) red pepper flakes

10 ml (2 tsp) sesame oil

15 ml (1 tbsp) rice vinegar

45 ml (3 tbsp) chopped fresh coriander

Method

1
Peel thin strips off the cucumber for a green and white striped effect.

2
Cut in half lengthways, or in quarters if the cucumber is thick.

3
Cut each length into 5-cm (2-in) pieces. Sprinkle with salt and leave to stand for 30 minutes. Wash and dry well on absorbent kitchen paper.

4
Combine the cucumber with all the remaining ingredients except the coriander in a deep bowl. Partially cover and cook in a microwave oven for 2 minutes on HIGH.

5
Stir in the coriander and leave in the bowl to cool. When cold, refrigerate. Serve on the same day.

Serving suggestion

Serve as a starter to a Chinese meal or as an accompaniment to cold or barbecued meat or poultry.

Variations

Use 2 large courgettes in place of cucumber. Use parsley or mint in place of coriander. Use chilli oil in place of sesame oil.

Cook's tip

Salting cucumbers helps to draw out excess moisture and keeps the dressing from becoming watery. It also makes cucumbers more digestible.

Sweet-Sour Cabbage

Shredded cabbage gets a sweet-and-sour treatment with light brown sugar and the zip of chilli pepper in this Oriental relish.

Preparation time: 20 minutes • Cooking time: 5-10 minutes • Serves: 4

Ingredients

1 medium white cabbage, weighing about 900 g (2 lb)

1 small red chilli, or to taste

115 g (4 oz) light brown sugar

90 ml (6 tbsp) rice vinegar

30 ml (2 tbsp) light soy sauce

Salt

45 ml (3 tbsp) vegetable oil

Method

1. Shred the cabbage into 1-cm (½-in) slices, discarding the core, and set aside.
2. Cut the chilli into short, thin strips, discarding the seeds.
3. Mix all the remaining ingredients together, except the oil, in a bowl.
4. Heat the oil in a wok or large frying pan. Add the cabbage mixture and stir-fry over a medium heat for 5-10 minutes, until just cooked and tender.
5. Set aside to cool, then cover and refrigerate before serving.

Serving suggestion

Serve as a side dish to an Oriental main course, or serve with boiled rice as a light meal.

Variations

Use red or green cabbage in place of white cabbage. Use dry sherry in place of rice vinegar.

Cook's tip

The cabbage will keep for several days if stored in its liquid in the refrigerator.

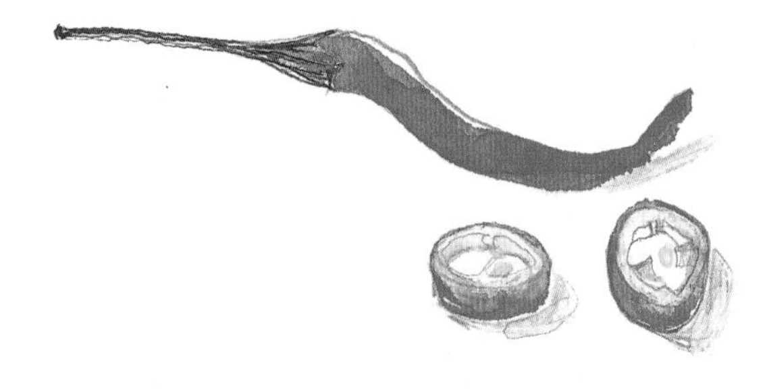

Sesame Stir-Fry

This recipe can be prepared in advance and cooked quickly for a romantic Oriental meal for two.

Preparation time: 15 minutes • Cooking time: 15 minutes (microwave on HIGH) • Serves: 2

Ingredients

30 ml (2 tbsp) vegetable oil

2.5 ml (1/2 tsp) finely chopped root ginger

15 g (1/2 oz) sesame seeds

55 g (2 oz) mangetout

1 stick celery, sliced

2 baby corn cobs, halved lengthways

55 g (2 oz) water chestnuts, thinly sliced diagonally

30 g (1 oz) button mushrooms, thinly sliced

1 spring onion, sliced diagonally

1 small red pepper, seeded and thinly sliced

115 g (4 oz) Chinese leaves, shredded

115 g (4 oz) fresh bean sprouts

15 g (1/2 oz) cornflour

30 ml (2 tbsp) soy sauce

15 ml (1 tbsp) sherry

2.5 ml (1/2 tsp) sesame oil

Method

1

Heat a browning dish in a microwave oven for 5 minutes on HIGH.

2

Place the vegetable oil on the browning dish and add the ginger and sesame seeds. Cook on HIGH for 30 seconds, then stir well.

3

Add the mangetout, celery, baby corn cobs, water chestnuts, mushrooms, spring onion and pepper. Stir well to coat with the oil, then cook for 4 minutes on HIGH, stirring well after each minute to brown the vegetables evenly.

4

Toss in the Chinese leaves and bean sprouts. Stir well and cook for a further 1 minute on HIGH.

5

In a small bowl, mix the cornflour with the soy sauce, sherry, sesame oil and 60 ml (4 tbsp) water, to form a smooth liquid.

6

Cover the bowl with cling film and pierce several times with the tip of a sharp knife. Cook the sauce on HIGH for 1-2 minutes, or until smooth and clear, stirring once or twice.

7

Pour the sauce over the vegetables in the browning dish and stir well to coat evenly.

8

Heat through for 1 minute on HIGH before serving.

Serving suggestion

Serve with boiled herb- or saffron-flavoured rice.

Variations

Use any combination of vegetables of your choice. Use garlic in place of ginger.

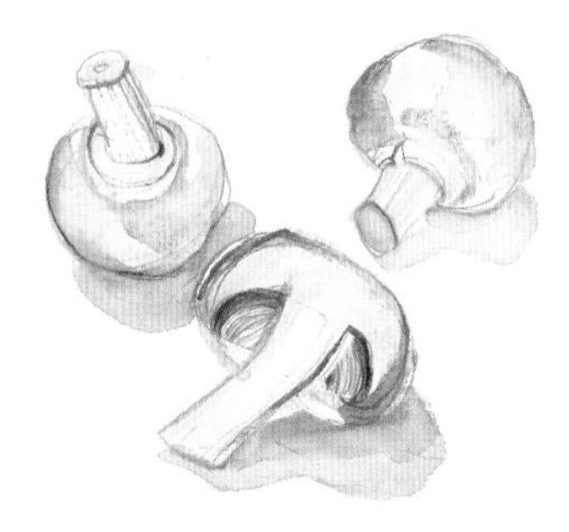

Banana Fritters

These delicious fritters make the perfect end to a spicy Oriental meal, and are much loved by children and adults alike.

Preparation time: 20 minutes, plus 1 hour standing time • Cooking time: 10 minutes • Serves: 4

Ingredients

175 g (6 oz) plain flour
5 ml (1 tsp) dried easy-blend yeast
125 ml (4 fl oz) warm milk
2 pinches of salt
1 egg
30 ml (2 tbsp) sunflower oil
2 bananas
Vegetable oil, for deep-frying
Icing sugar
Ground cinnamon

Method

1
Place the flour in a bowl and mix in the yeast and the warm milk. Stir in the salt, egg and the sunflower oil. Mix well to make a thick but light batter. Leave to rest in a warm place for 1 hour.

2
Peel the bananas, slice each in half lengthways, then twice crossways, to make 6 pieces from each banana.

3
Heat the vegetable oil for deep-frying. Dip each banana piece in the batter, then drop into the hot oil.

4
Turn the fritters over during cooking. When the fritters are crisp and golden, drain on absorbent kitchen paper, sift over a mixture of icing sugar and cinnamon and serve immediately.

Serving suggestion

Serve with crème fraîche or whipped cream.

Variations

Use other fruit such as apples, pears or pineapple in place of bananas. Use ground mixed spice or ginger in place of cinnamon.

Cook's tip

The oil should be hot enough to cook the fritters through without burning the outside.

Tapioca with Golden Threads

In Oriental cooking, golden threads are used to decorate desserts, as in this case, or enjoyed on their own with coffee.

Preparation time: 20 minutes • Cooking time: 45 minutes • Serves: 6

Ingredients

For the golden threads

6 egg yolks

280 g (10 oz) granulated sugar

For the tapioca

600 ml (1 pint) thin coconut milk *(see 'Cook's tip', page 40)*

85 g (3 oz) pearl tapioca, rinsed

25 g (1 oz) palm sugar

Method

1
To make the golden threads, puncture the base of a paper or plastic cup 3 or 4 times with a knitting needle or skewer.

2
Stir the egg yolks together and leave in the refrigerator until required.

3
Place 300 ml (½ pint) water and granulated sugar in a wok or saucepan and heat, stirring, until the sugar dissolves. Bring to the boil, then reduce the heat to maintain a gentle boil.

4
Pour about ⅓-½ of the egg yolk mixture into the cup while holding it over the saucepan of sugar and water. Let the yolks flow through the holes in the cup, in a steady stream. Move the cup slowly from side to side, so that the yolk forms strings.

5
As the yolk mixture hits the water it will cook. When set, remove with a skewer, fold into bundles and place on a plate. Repeat with the remaining egg, then cool and chill until required. Discard the sugar syrup.

6
To make the tapioca, place the coconut milk and tapioca in a saucepan, stir in the palm sugar and cook over a low heat for about 30 minutes, stirring occasionally, until the tapioca is tender. Spoon into dishes and arrange the golden threads on top. Serve.

Serving suggestion
Serve with fresh sliced fruit such as strawberries and kiwi fruit. Serve any spare golden threads with coffee.

Variations
Use pudding rice or semolina in place of tapioca. Add the finely grated rind of 1 lemon or 1 small orange to the tapioca mixture.

Cook's tip
Palm sugar is a thick brown sugar made from the boiled sap of the palmyra palm tree or the coconut palm. It is almost wet in texture, and is available in tubs or cans from Oriental stores. Substitute an unrefined sugar, such as light or dark muscovado sugar, if unavailable.

Mango Bricks

Filo pastry encloses a tangy, fruit-flavoured filling to make a dessert that tastes perfect after a rich meal.

Preparation time: 20 minutes • Cooking time: 15 minutes • Serves: 4

Ingredients

225 ml (8 fl oz) milk
2 egg yolks
38 ml (2½ tbsp) granulated sugar
23 ml (1½ tbsp) plain flour, sifted
15 ml (1 tbsp) coconut liqueur
1 ripe mango
4 sheets filo pastry
3 kiwi fruit
30 ml (2 tbsp) caster sugar
15 ml (1 tbsp) butter
60 ml (4 tbsp) raspberry purée
Fresh mint sprigs, to decorate

Method

1
Place the milk in a saucepan and bring to the boil. Beat together the egg yolks and granulated sugar until the mixture is light and lemon coloured. Add the flour and mix in well.

2
Pour the boiling milk over the egg mixture, then return it to the saucepan and cook until thickened, stirring continuously. Remove the pan from the heat and set aside to cool.

3
When the pastry cream is cool, mix in the coconut liqueur. Set aside.

4
Peel and stone the mango and cut the flesh into slices or small pieces.

5
Spread 15 ml (1 tbsp) of the pastry cream onto each sheet of filo pastry to cover. Place the mango in the centre of the filo sheets.

6
Fold in each side of the filo up and over the mango. Fold in the top and bottom. Set the 4 even-sized 'bricks' aside until ready for cooking.

7
Peel the kiwi fruit and remove the white core. Place the flesh in a food processor with the caster sugar and 60 ml (4 tbsp) water and mix to a smooth purée. Chill in the refrigerator until required.

8
Heat the butter in a pan until melted and golden brown, add the 'bricks' and fry for about 2½ minutes on each side, until golden.

9
Place the cooked 'bricks' on serving plates and serve with the kiwi fruit and raspberry purées. Decorate with fresh mint sprigs.

Serving suggestion
Serve with thick cream, crème fraîche or Greek yogurt.

Variations
Use bananas, papaya or pineapple in place of mango. Use peaches in place of kiwi fruit.

Cook's tip
The creamy filling sweats a little when spread on the filo pastry. This helps to keep the pastry damp.

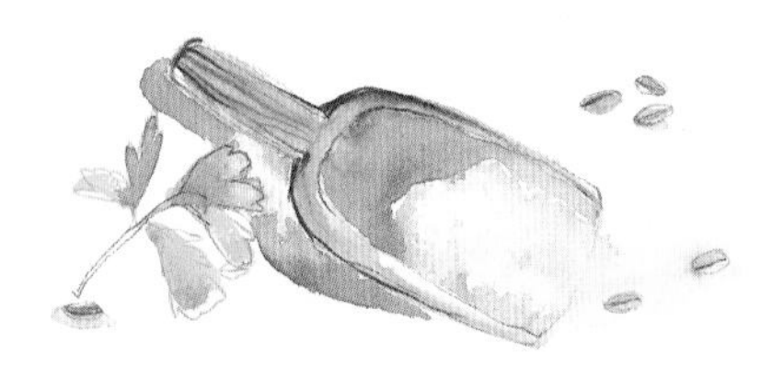

Bananas in Coconut Milk

You can use small, hard Thai bananas for this dish. If so, increase the cooking time so that the banana is cooked until just tender.

Preparation time: 10 minutes • Cooking time: 12 minutes • Serves: 6

Ingredients

600 ml (1 pint) thin coconut milk
(see 'Cook's tip', page 40)

115 g (4 oz) caster sugar

A pinch of salt

6 small bananas

Toasted desiccated coconut, to decorate

Method

1
Combine the coconut milk, sugar and salt in a wok or saucepan and heat gently, stirring, until the sugar dissolves. Bring to the boil and boil rapidly for 5 minutes.

2
Peel and cut the bananas in half or into chunks and place in the coconut milk. Reduce the heat and simmer gently for 2-3 minutes, or until the bananas are just soft.

3
Allow the mixture to cool and serve slightly warm or cold, sprinkled with the desiccated coconut.

Serving suggestion

Serve with sponge fingers or wafer biscuits.

Variations

Use fresh pineapple in place of bananas. Use soft brown sugar in place of caster sugar. Sprinkle with grated nutmeg or ground cinnamon before serving.

Cook's tip

Choose slightly green bananas for this dish.

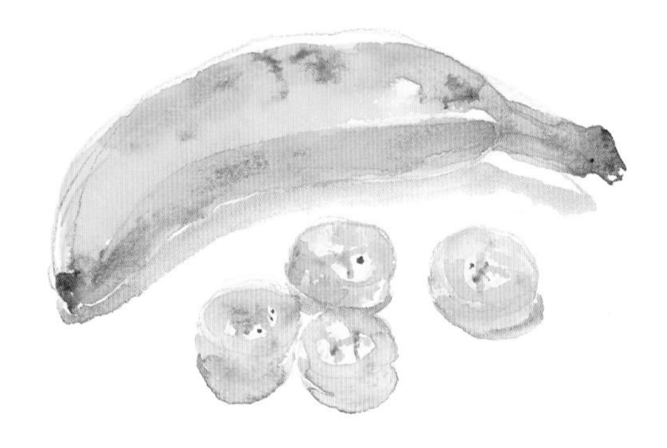

Sweet Fruit Pilau

Fragrantly spiced and served with fresh fruit, this unusual dessert is a delicious way of serving rice.

Preparation time: 25 minutes • Cooking time: 15 minutes, plus standing time (microwave on HIGH) • Serves: 6

Ingredients

55 g (2 oz) vegetable margarine

225 g (8 oz) pudding rice

25 g (1 oz) cashew nuts

25 g (1 oz) flaked almonds

600 ml (1 pint) hot milk

115 g (4 oz) caster sugar

9 cardamoms, lightly crushed

4 cloves

2.5 ml (1/2 tsp) grated nutmeg

Finely grated rind of 1 orange

A few drops of orange flower water

55 g (2 oz) black sesame seeds

1 small mango, peeled, stoned and sliced

55 g (2 oz) white grapes, halved, seeded and peeled

1 orange, peeled and segmented

1 kiwi fruit, peeled and sliced

Method

1
Place the margarine, rice and nuts in a large, deep bowl and cook, uncovered, on HIGH for 3 minutes.

2
Stir the rice mixture once or twice during the cooking time to ensure that the nuts become evenly browned.

3
Pour the milk onto the rice mixture and stir in the sugar until it has dissolved.

4
Add the cardamoms, cloves, nutmeg, orange rind and orange flower water.

5
Cover the bowl with cling film and pierce several times with the tip of a sharp knife.

6
Cook the rice for 12 minutes on HIGH, stirring occasionally to prevent it from sticking.

7
Allow the rice to stand for 5 minutes, then stir in the sesame seeds.

8
Spoon the rice into a serving dish and decorate with the prepared fruit before serving hot or cold.

Serving suggestion

Serve with sponge biscuits or wafer biscuits.

Variations

Use any fresh fruit of your choice, such as bananas, pineapple, strawberries and peaches. Use hazelnuts or pecan nuts in place of cashew nuts. Use ground mixed spice or ginger in place of nutmeg.

Sticky Rice with Mango and Star Fruit

In this rich dish, glutinous rice is combined with thick coconut milk and sugar and served with exotic fruits.

Preparation time: 10 minutes, plus soaking time overnight • Cooking time: 27 minutes, plus 15 minutes standing time • Serves: 4

Ingredients

225 g (8 oz) glutinous rice

425 ml (¾ pint) thick coconut milk *(see 'Cook's tip', page 40)*

85 g (3 oz) sugar

A pinch of salt

1 mango

1 star fruit

Method

1
Soak the rice overnight in a bowl of cold water.

2
Line the top of a steamer with muslin. Drain the rice and place in a steamer. Cover and steam for 25 minutes. The rice should be just tender but not fully cooked.

3
Combine the coconut milk, sugar and salt in a saucepan and heat gently. Stir in the steamed rice and simmer for 2 minutes.

4
Remove from the heat, cover and leave to stand for 15 minutes. The rice will continue to cook in this time.

5
Cut the mango in half as close to the stone as possible. Remove and discard the stone and peel and slice the flesh. Slice the star fruit crossways.

6
Arrange the fruit and rice attractively on serving dishes and serve.

Serving suggestion

Serve with thick Greek yogurt or crème fraîche.

Variations

Use other prepared fresh fruit, such as papaya and kiwi fruit, in place of the mango and star fruit. Add cinnamon or nutmeg, or grated orange or lemon rind to the rice before serving.

Index